what would your contemporary art project proposal be if you were invited by a curator to participate in a contemporary art exhibition?

an artist's book by
anonymous stranger

what would your contemporary art project proposal be if you were invited by a curator to participate in a contemporary art exhibition? is an artist's book by *anonymous stranger* with texts compiled from anonymous strangers at Omegle spy chat (www.omegle.com) responding to the question posed in the title of this book.
http://anonymousstranger.httpdot.net/thebook

what would your contemporary art project proposal be if you were invited by a curator to participate in a contemporary art exhibition?
no copyright. dedicated to public domain by *anonymous stranger*, 2013
ISBN: 978-1-304-53715-7

all texts by anonymous strangers (with nicknames stranger 1 & stranger 2) at Omegle spy chat are compiled by *anonymous stranger,* who also asked the question to be discussed, in various sessions between august 2011 and may 2013 and these texts (chat logs) are used in this book as is, without proof reading and modification. Omegle is an online anonymous chat service by Omegle.com LLC. spy mode at Omegle lets an anonymous stranger just ask a question and watch two anonymous strangers discuss it until one leaves the conversation. any of the anonymous strangers may save and share the log of the conversation.

this work is created entirely with free/libre software and designed by *anonymous stranger* with LibreOffice 3.5.7.2 using the typefaces GNU FreeFont and Anonymous Pro on GNU/Linux (Ubuntu 12.04 (precise) 64-bit) Ubuntu by Canonical Ltd, ubuntu community (GNU GPL and other FLOSS licenses) LibreOffice 3.5.7.2 by The Document Foundation, Debian and Ubuntu, based on OpenOffice.org by Oracle and/or its affiliates (GNU LGPLv3) GNUFreeFont by Free Software Foundation(GNU GPL) Anonymous Pro 1.002 by Mark Simonson (OFL)

what would
your contemporary art
project proposal be
if you were invited
by a curator
to participate in a
contemporary art
exhibition?

an artist's book by
anonymous stranger

anonymous stranger asked the question

"what would your contemporary art project proposal be if you were invited by a curator to participate in a contemporary art exhibition?"

to anonymous strangers
using spy chat mode of Omegle
in various sessions between
august 2011 and may 2013
and compiled the texts of
discussions on this question.

Question to discuss:
what would your contemporary art project proposal be
if you were invited by a curator to participate in a
contemporary art exhibition?
Stranger 1: WHAT?
Stranger 1 has disconnected

Question to discuss:
what would your contemporary art project proposal be
if you were invited by a curator to participate in a
contemporary art exhibition?
Stranger 2: i would have a single toothbrush
Stranger 1: long words why
Stranger 2: hanging from the sky
Stranger 1: omg
Stranger 2: from a piece of floss
Stranger 1: dfsgj
Stranger 2: everyone would claim i was a
          genius
Stranger 2: and i would marry johnny depp
          and live with him on a secluded
          island forever
Stranger 1: oh
Stranger 2: thank you
Stranger 1: ok
Stranger 1 has disconnected

Question to discuss:
what would your contemporary art project proposal be
if you were invited by a curator to participate in a
contemporary art exhibition?
Stranger 2: **stop making us do your homework**
Stranger 2 has disconnected

Question to discuss:
what would your contemporary art project proposal be
if you were invited by a curator to participate in a
contemporary art exhibition?

Stranger 1: i would invite everyone
Stranger 1: get them there
Stranger 2: **I actually think this is a creative question, thank you.**
Stranger 1: and then interrupt it with some techie guys
Stranger 1: busting up in there
Stranger 1: running cat5 cable and stuff
Stranger 1: getting in everyone's way
Stranger 2: **Until Stranger bgan speaking nonsense...**
Stranger 2: ***began**
Stranger 1: taking 5 hours
Stranger 1: to configure new software and stuff
Stranger 1: and it would be called
Stranger 1: INSTALLATION
Stranger 2: **You must be a computer person, aren't you?**
Stranger 2: **Ouch.**
Stranger 2: **Contemporary art is for artists.**
Stranger 1: oh ok
Stranger 1: the art part was throwing me off
Stranger 2: **Clearly, don't worry about it. You still did your best.**
Stranger 1: you sure are close-minded for an artist
Stranger 1: did you even understand my joke?
Stranger 1: Installation art describes an artistic genre of three-dimensional works that are often site-specific and designed to transform a viewer's perception of a space. Generally, the term is applied to interior spaces, whereas exterior interventions are often called Land art;

however the boundaries between
these terms overlap.

Stranger 2: **Close minded. I did not say I am
an artist.**

Stranger 2: **And,**

Stranger 2: **You proved me wrong.**

Stranger 2: **So bravo.**

Stranger 2: **I am impressed.**

Stranger 1 has disconnected

Question to discuss:
what would your contemporary art project proposal be
if you were invited by a curator to participate in a
contemporary art exhibition?

Stranger 1: Let me think for a moment…
            stranger can go first
**Stranger 2: Live girls playing with them
            selfs**
Stranger 1: An inverted cross with 2 nuns
            wearing close to nothing kissing
            themselves.
Stranger 1: Perhaps Jesus on the cross, not
            sure
Stranger 1: It would reppresent religious
            oppression
Stranger 2 has disconnected

Question to discuss:
what would your contemporary art project proposal be
if you were invited by a curator to participate in a
contemporary art exhibition?
Stranger 2: i have no idea what that is
Stranger 1 has disconnected

Question to discuss:
what would your contemporary art project proposal be
if you were invited by a curator to participate in a
contemporary art exhibition?
Stranger 2: what?
Stranger 2: i dont get it
Stranger 2: confusing!!!!!!
Stranger 1: Idon'tunderstand.
Stranger 2 has disconnected

Question to discuss:
what would your contemporary art project proposal be
if you were invited by a curator to participate in a
contemporary art exhibition?
Stranger 2: hippies
Stranger 1: i don't even understand that
Stranger 2: lol same
Stranger 1: heh
Stranger 2: I saw it earlier and some
british queer explained it to me
Stranger 2: only a brit would know what it
means.
Stranger 2 has disconnected

Question to discuss:
what would your contemporary art project proposal be
if you were invited by a curator to participate in a
contemporary art exhibition?
Stranger 2: euh
Stranger 2: wait
Stranger 1: sounds too much like an
           extraordinarily shitty artist
           asking for help
Stranger 1 has disconnected

Question to discuss:
what would your contemporary art project proposal be
if you were invited by a curator to participate in a
contemporary art exhibition?

Stranger 1: idk
Stranger 1: i am in an art school
Stranger 1: but i don't do contemporary
Stranger 1: :/ i'm still at the stage where
            they let us do whatever the heel
            we want
Stranger 2: **i'd probably masturbate on my
            dog and make him stand in the
            exhibition**
Stranger 1: my art teacher would love that
            idea!
Stranger 1: :D
Stranger 1: thats great
Stranger 1: you should becoome an artist
Stranger 2: **ok, well you can have it, go
            impress her**
Stranger 1: you have so much potential
Stranger 1: not
Stranger 1: go fuck yourself
Stranger 1 has disconnected

Question to discuss:
what would your contemporary art project proposal be
if you were invited by a curator to participate in a
contemporary art exhibition?
Stranger 2: no
Stranger 1 has disconnected

Question to discuss:
what would your contemporary art project proposal be
if you were invited by a curator to participate in a
contemporary art exhibition?
Stranger 1: I no understand.
Stranger 2: **i'm a real scientist so i don't
know**
Stranger 1: Lol.
Stranger 1 has disconnected

Question to discuss:
what would your contemporary art project proposal be
if you were invited by a curator to participate in a
contemporary art exhibition?
Stranger 2: Lolwut?
Stranger 2 has disconnected

Question to discuss:
what would your contemporary art project proposal be
if you were invited by a curator to participate in a
contemporary art exhibition?

Stranger 1: I would throw stones at a
painting
Stranger 1: and say it's the end of modern
art
Stranger 1: then i'd shoot paper stars from
a papermaché bum
Stranger 1: which is painted purple
Stranger 2: **That's a way better idea than I
was gonna say**
Stranger 1: I know, art is so easy
Stranger 1 has disconnected

Question to discuss:
what would your contemporary art project proposal be
if you were invited by a curator to participate in a
contemporary art exhibition?
Stranger 2: **WHAT?**
Stranger 2: **o_o**
Stranger 1: it would be
Stranger 1: lke this
Stranger 2 has disconnected

Question to discuss:
what would your contemporary art project proposal be
if you were invited by a curator to participate in a
contemporary art exhibition?
Stranger 1: a buddha
Stranger 2 has disconnected

Question to discuss:
what would your contemporary art project proposal be
if you were invited by a curator to participate in a
contemporary art exhibition?
Stranger 2: **The art of not giving a fuck**
Stranger 1: idk
Stranger 1 has disconnected

Question to discuss:
what would your contemporary art project proposal be
if you were invited by a curator to participate in a
contemporary art exhibition?
Stranger 1 has disconnected

Question to discuss:

what would your contemporary art project proposal be
if you were invited by a curator to participate in a
contemporary art exhibition?

Stranger 1: BRAINY

Stranger 2: **a syringe full of moldy custard**

Stranger 1 has disconnected

Question to discuss:
what would your contemporary art project proposal be
if you were invited by a curator to participate in a
contemporary art exhibition?
Stranger 2: no
Stranger 1: I would make a machine that
          flies around and spits at people
Stranger 1: and then farts rainbows
Stranger 2 has disconnected

Question to discuss:
what would your contemporary art project proposal be
if you were invited by a curator to participate in a
contemporary art exhibition?

Stranger 2: **what**
Stranger 1: lol
Stranger 2: **not even gonna finish reading that shit**
Stranger 1: well im not good with creative things
Stranger 1: so ill probably think something on wine
Stranger 1: or women
Stranger 1: thats more of a practical approach for me
Stranger 2: **lol just do drugs and it'll come to you**
Stranger 2: **I recomend heroin**
Stranger 1: no
Stranger 2: **recommend***
Stranger 1: im not a druggie
Stranger 1: well cigs and alcohol works for me
Stranger 2: **I was talking to the guy who asked the question lol**
Stranger 1: lol
Stranger 2: **I like cigs, but I always throw up on the girl I'm trying to bone when I'm drunk**
Stranger 1: ya creative people are druggies
Stranger 2: **lol yeah**
Stranger 1: so u can plan
Stranger 1: perfect match i guess
Stranger 1: hahaha
Stranger 2: **haha straigh tup**
Stranger 2: **dude I want some mashed potatoes**
Stranger 2: **with butter**
Stranger 2: **mm**
Stranger 1: well thats not my thing ya
Stranger 1: im a guy so u can probably find a girl

Stranger 1: to do the household work

Stranger 1: :D

Stranger 2: I've found a few, but for some reason they don't like it when you puke on them lol

Stranger 2: ohh haha xD

Stranger 1: ya its disgusting actually

Stranger 2: I don't even know what you're talking about to be honest

Stranger 2: I just type shit

Stranger 2: haha

Stranger 1: so was i

Stranger 1: this is internet so it doesnt matter what u say or think

Stranger 2: yeah

Stranger 2: I like little boys

Stranger 2: haha

Stranger 1: pedo

Stranger 2: lol pedo bear

Stranger 1: im a man not a boy

Stranger 1: sorry hard luck

Stranger 2: oh you're to old for me, I like them before the grass begins to grow

Stranger 2: you know what's fun?

Stranger 1: i definately know whats fun more than u :D

Stranger 2: raping old woman? yeah I know, it's a hoot

Stranger 1: whats your asl anyway ?

Stranger 2: oh

Stranger 2: it's

Stranger 1: lol

Stranger 1: id never do that

Stranger 2: 16, male, califoria. And lol neither would I, I'm just fucking around

Stranger 2: cuz it's OmEgLe!

Stranger 1 has disconnected

Question to discuss:

what would your contemporary art project proposal be
if you were invited by a curator to participate in a
contemporary art exhibition?

Stranger 1: DIE

Stranger 2: **DO YOUR OWN DAMN WORK**

Stranger 1: DIE

Stranger 2 has disconnected

Question to discuss:
what would your contemporary art project proposal be
if you were invited by a curator to participate in a
contemporary art exhibition?
Stranger 2: **i would shit on the floor**
Stranger 1: I would take a wshit on the
curator and call it art
Stranger 2: **it would be a commentary on how
shitty contemporary art is**
Stranger 2 has disconnected

Question to discuss:
what would your contemporary art project proposal be
if you were invited by a curator to participate in a
contemporary art exhibition?
Stranger 1: Draw a dinosaur.
Stranger 2 has disconnected

Question to discuss:
what would your contemporary art project proposal be
if you were invited by a curator to participate in a
contemporary art exhibition?
Stranger 2:

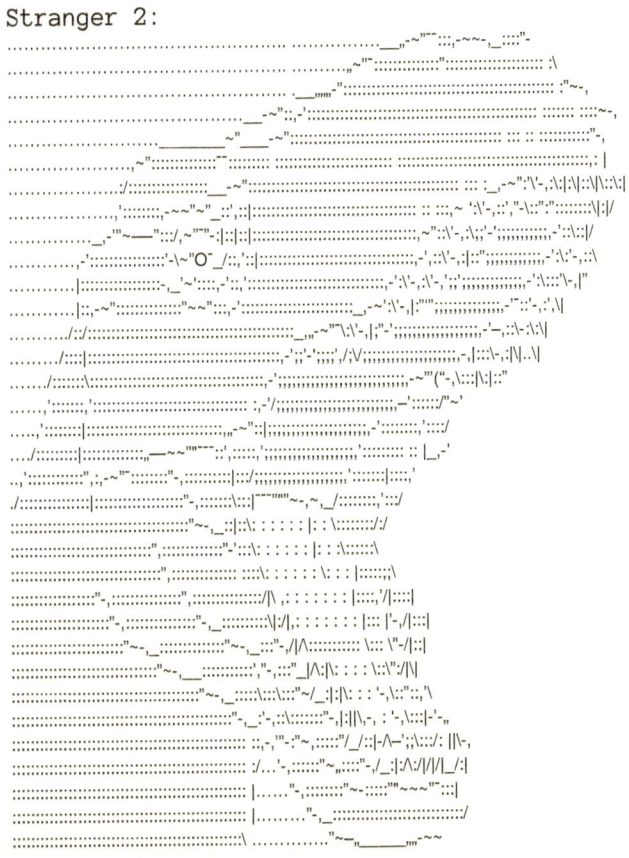

Stranger 2 has disconnected

Question to discuss:
what would your contemporary art project proposal be
if you were invited by a curator to participate in a
contemporary art exhibition?
Stranger 1: Doggy Style sculpture of the
Queen and A Fluffy hatted
soldier
Stranger 1: *english queen
Stranger 1: LONG DIE MONARCHY
Stranger 1 has disconnected

Question to discuss:
what would your contemporary art project proposal be
if you were invited by a curator to participate in a
contemporary art exhibition?

Stranger 1: This is a horrible place to ask
such a question.

Stranger 2: I've got some drawings I made
while tweaked out of my mind…

Stranger 2: They're pretty bizaare to look
at.

Stranger 2: Might be worth an exhibit.

Stranger 1: Sounds like my family.

Stranger 1 has disconnected

Question to discuss:
what would your contemporary art project proposal be
if you were invited by a curator to participate in a
contemporary art exhibition?
Stranger 2: **FUCKIN|G**
Stranger 2 has disconnected

Question to discuss:
what would your contemporary art project proposal be
if you were invited by a curator to participate in a
contemporary art exhibition?
Stranger 1: hææ ?
Stranger 2: **contemporary**
Stranger 2 has disconnected

Question to discuss:
what would your contemporary art project proposal be
if you were invited by a curator to participate in a
contemporary art exhibition?
Stranger 2: A Budah submersed in pee
Stranger 2: Full size
Stranger 1: i thought poo, but then you
            wouldnt see the buddha
Stranger 2: yeah
Stranger 2: Transend this you taoist basterd
Stranger 2: *wiz*
Stranger 1 has disconnected

Question to discuss:
what would your contemporary art project proposal be
if you were invited by a curator to participate in a
contemporary art exhibition?

Stranger 2: **im not an artist so i cant help**
you

Stranger 1: Er…

Stranger 2: **maybe just spread some paint**
around on a page and call it
"art"

Stranger 1: Considering modern art

Stranger 1: Probably a nice turd I found
pretty inside a toilet.

Stranger 1: Then varnish the whole deal.

Stranger 2: **lol XD**

Stranger 2: **too true. modern art is a joke**

Stranger 2 has disconnected

Question to discuss:
what would your contemporary art project proposal be
if you were invited by a curator to participate in a
contemporary art exhibition?
Stranger 1: the passage of time
Stranger 2: "Why Apple Pie Does not Fit Up
my Anus, subtitle: A Brief
Exploration of The Artist's
Anus.
Stranger 1 has disconnected

Question to discuss:
what would your contemporary art project proposal be
if you were invited by a curator to participate in a
contemporary art exhibition?
Stranger 2: **a painting of my bf with
anything but paint**
Stranger 2 has disconnected

Question to discuss:

what would your contemporary art project proposal be if you were invited by a curator to participate in a contemporary art exhibition?

Stranger 1: make a bunch of pottery and then run in and smash them one by one

Stranger 1: have security chase me and everything

Stranger 1 has disconnected

Question to discuss:
what would your contemporary art project proposal be
if you were invited by a curator to participate in a
contemporary art exhibition?
Stranger 1: yes
Stranger 1 has disconnected

Question to discuss:
what would your contemporary art project proposal be
if you were invited by a curator to participate in a
contemporary art exhibition?
Stranger 2: SPAM
Stranger 1: A big pencil because wtf
Stranger 2 has disconnected

Question to discuss:
what would your contemporary art project proposal be
if you were invited by a curator to participate in a
contemporary art exhibition?
Stranger 2: **cheater**
Stranger 1 has disconnected

Question to discuss:
what would your contemporary art project proposal be
if you were invited by a curator to participate in a
contemporary art exhibition?
Stranger 2: **wut**
Stranger 2: **idk**
Stranger 2: **sorry** ;P
Stranger 2 has disconnected

Question to discuss:
what would your contemporary art project proposal be
if you were invited by a curator to participate in a
contemporary art exhibition?
Stranger 2: **I like those fancy words. They
make me giggle.**
Stranger 1: Well, I would take the
physiological you and throw it
Stranger 1: … xD What..
Stranger 2: **xxD**
Stranger 2 has disconnected

Question to discuss:
what would your contemporary art project proposal be
if you were invited by a curator to participate in a
contemporary art exhibition?
Stranger 1: it would be
Stranger 1: a massive pile of sand
Stranger 1: thats it.
Stranger 2: mine would be the different
            colours of wee that your wee
            goes when you eat/drink certain
            things
Stranger 1: thats a good one
Stranger 1: like in seperate vials?
Stranger 2: yep, it'd be in test tubes all
            lined up
Stranger 1: cool man
Stranger 2: and people would have to guess
            what the person had eaten/drank
            for it do go that shade of
            yellow
Stranger 1 has disconnected

Question to discuss:
what would your contemporary art project proposal be
if you were invited by a curator to participate in a
contemporary art exhibition?
Stranger 1: idk what this means
Stranger 1 has disconnected

Question to discuss:
what would your contemporary art project proposal be
if you were invited by a curator to participate in a
contemporary art exhibition?
Stranger 2: **Dicks man**
Stranger 1 has disconnected

Question to discuss:
what would your contemporary art project proposal be
if you were invited by a curator to participate in a
contemporary art exhibition?
Stranger 2: **video games**
Stranger 1 has disconnected

Question to discuss:
what would your contemporary art project proposal be
if you were invited by a curator to participate in a
contemporary art exhibition?
Stranger 1: What's curator?
Stranger 1 has disconnected

Question to discuss:
what would your contemporary art project proposal be
if you were invited by a curator to participate in a
contemporary art exhibition?
Stranger 2: dont know
Stranger 2: if you need tips
Stranger 2: why ask here
Stranger 2 has disconnected

Question to discuss:
what would your contemporary art project proposal be
if you were invited by a curator to participate in a
contemporary art exhibition?
Stranger 2: **Wow, I like this question**
Stranger 1: hello
Stranger 1: you m/f
Stranger 2: **M**
Stranger 1 has disconnected

Question to discuss:
what would your contemporary art project proposal be
if you were invited by a curator to participate in a
contemporary art exhibition?
Stranger 1: um no hippie
Stranger 1 has disconnected

Question to discuss:
what would your contemporary art project proposal be
if you were invited by a curator to participate in a
contemporary art exhibition?
Stranger 2: **most contemporary art is shit**
Stranger 2 has disconnected

```
Question to discuss:
```
what would your contemporary art project proposal be
if you were invited by a curator to participate in a
contemporary art exhibition?
```
Stranger 2: sex
Stranger 1: yes
Stranger 1: asl?
Stranger 2 has disconnected
```

Question to discuss:
what would your contemporary art project proposal be
if you were invited by a curator to participate in a
contemporary art exhibition?
Stranger 1: what the..?
Stranger 2: I LOVE NIGGERS
Stranger 1: ^^^
Stranger 2: Seppel1968
Stranger 1: yes.
Stranger 2 has disconnected

Question to discuss:
what would your contemporary art project proposal be
if you were invited by a curator to participate in a
contemporary art exhibition?

Stranger 1: How about
Stranger 1: Eagles talons shaped into a
middle finger
Stranger 2: ^ Best idea.
Stranger 1: I win the million dollars.
Stranger 2: I SHIT YOU NOT
Stranger 1: :D
Stranger 2: You have won family fued
stranger
Stranger 1: Why thank you
Stranger 2: You are very welcome
Stranger 1: Agh shit
Stranger 2: Shit what?
Stranger 1: I hear mice in my walls ;(
Stranger 1: I HATE MICE
Stranger 2: CALL EXTERMINATOR
Stranger 1: Yeah… They suck
Stranger 2: o-o Imagine if they are rats
Stranger 1: They're mice.
Stranger 2: BIG FUCKING RATS IN YOUR WALLS,
JUST IMAGINE THAT
Stranger 1: Nasty man
Stranger 2: And harder to remoe
Stranger 1: Like the ending of 1984
Stranger 2: *remove
Stranger 1: And fucking huge
Stranger 2: And I love you random citizen
Stranger 2: HAVE A NICE DAY :D
Stranger 2 has disconnected

Question to discuss:
what would your contemporary art project proposal be
if you were invited by a curator to participate in a
contemporary art exhibition?
Stranger 1: how do you know if a piece of
            art is contempotary?
Stranger 2 has disconnected

Question to discuss:
what would your contemporary art project proposal be
if you were invited by a curator to participate in a
contemporary art exhibition?
Stranger 2: **an exhibition of pencils**
Stranger 2 has disconnected

Question to discuss:

what would your contemporary art project proposal be if you were invited by a curator to participate in a contemporary art exhibition?

Stranger 2: **curator? arent those the things that make coffee and such?**

Stranger 1: what you can do in a art project?

Stranger 2 has disconnected

Question to discuss:
what would your contemporary art project proposal be
if you were invited by a curator to participate in a
contemporary art exhibition?
Stranger 2: **blue canvas with black speck**
Stranger 2: **done.**
Stranger 2: **:)**
Stranger 1 has disconnected

Question to discuss:
what would your contemporary art project proposal be
if you were invited by a curator to participate in a
contemporary art exhibition?
Stranger 2: **No**.
Stranger 2 has disconnected

Question to discuss:
what would your contemporary art project proposal be
if you were invited by a curator to participate in a
contemporary art exhibition?
Stranger 2: **i dont get art**
Stranger 2 has disconnected

Question to discuss:
what would your contemporary art project proposal be
if you were invited by a curator to participate in a
contemporary art exhibition?

Stranger 2: um
Stranger 1: wat.
Stranger 1: a dinosaur! :D
Stranger 2: i'd pee on a canvas
Stranger 1: made of toothpicks. >:)
Stranger 2: then submit it to the art
            exhibition
Stranger 2: and say it's art
Stranger 1: not piss
Stranger 1: xD.
Stranger 2: then I'd say it's better than
            all the other painters out there
            today
Stranger 1: ^so true^
Stranger 2: and how the hell does the
            curator not enjoy my
            contemporary art
Stranger 1: yep.
Stranger 2: it relates to the experience of
            the youth
Stranger 2: and the hardship and struggles
            of life
Stranger 2: so piss on it
Stranger 1: because its the law
Stranger 2: yessir
Stranger 1: i'd piss on a canvas.
Stranger 1: if i had to
Stranger 1: ya know…'
Stranger 2: cool story bro
Stranger 1: yup.
Stranger 1 has disconnected

Question to discuss:
what would your contemporary art project proposal be
if you were invited by a curator to participate in a
contemporary art exhibition?
Stranger 2: **Do your own work faggot.**
Stranger 2 has disconnected

Question to discuss:
what would your contemporary art project proposal be
if you were invited by a curator to participate in a
contemporary art exhibition?
Stranger 1: I don't understand art, so no
             idea
Stranger 2: **Me neither, sorry**
Stranger 2 has disconnected

Question to discuss:
what would your contemporary art project proposal be
if you were invited by a curator to participate in a
contemporary art exhibition?
Stranger 1: You mean make art?
Stranger 2: **um idk**
Stranger 1: I only knew some of those words.
Stranger 1: I suck at art.
Stranger 1: ;_;
Stranger 1 has disconnected

Question to discuss:
what would your contemporary art project proposal be
if you were invited by a curator to participate in a
contemporary art exhibition?
Stranger 2: **? what????**
Stranger 1: whaaaaa?
Stranger 2: **exactly**
Stranger 2: ..
Stranger 1 has disconnected

Question to discuss:
what would your contemporary art project proposal be
if you were invited by a curator to participate in a
contemporary art exhibition?
Stranger 2: **poo**
Stranger 2 has disconnected

Question to discuss:
what would your contemporary art project proposal be
if you were invited by a curator to participate in a
contemporary art exhibition?
Stranger 2: **I'd draw a dragon.**
Stranger 1: I don't even know what
contemporary art is
Stranger 1 has disconnected

Question to discuss:
what would your contemporary art project proposal be
if you were invited by a curator to participate in a
contemporary art exhibition?
Stranger 2: aha
Stranger 2: um
Stranger 1: i was already here..
Stranger 2: idk man i can't even create my
own art
Stranger 2: so i'm probably not going to be
much help with someone else's
Stranger 1: try using words people actually
know next time
Stranger 1 has disconnected

Question to discuss:
what would your contemporary art project proposal be
if you were invited by a curator to participate in a
contemporary art exhibition?
Stranger 2: **FIRE! And lots of it!**
Stranger 1 has disconnected

Question to discuss:
what would your contemporary art project proposal be
if you were invited by a curator to participate in a
contemporary art exhibition?
Stranger 1: Hmm…
Stranger 1: Build the eiffel tower out of
            French Fries…
Stranger 1: Is that considered contemporary?
Stranger 1 has disconnected

Question to discuss:
what would your contemporary art project proposal be
if you were invited by a curator to participate in a
contemporary art exhibition?
Stranger 1: what is art
Stranger 1 has disconnected

Question to discuss:
what would your contemporary art project proposal be
if you were invited by a curator to participate in a
contemporary art exhibition?
Stranger 1: FUCK YOU
Stranger 2: A giant golden dildo.
Stranger 1: art is for people that want to
               live on the street
Stranger 1: its not a job
Stranger 2: With big ass vibrator that makes
               it spin around and clean wooden
               floors like a zoomba
Stranger 1: ^ gay
Stranger 1 has disconnected

Question to discuss:
what would your contemporary art project proposal be
if you were invited by a curator to participate in a
contemporary art exhibition?
Stranger 1: lol dont steal our ideas
Stranger 2: **yeah!**
Stranger 2: **xD**
Stranger 1: come up with your own
Stranger 1 has disconnected

Question to discuss:
what would your contemporary art project proposal be
if you were invited by a curator to participate in a
contemporary art exhibition?
Stranger 1: what?
Stranger 2: **I will exibit the portrait of my
dick**
Stranger 1: sorry i cant understand
Stranger 1: asshole
Stranger 1 has disconnected

Question to discuss:
what would your contemporary art project proposal be
if you were invited by a curator to participate in a
contemporary art exhibition?
Stranger 1: rather exquisite
Stranger 2: I would choose a lawn chair
Stranger 1 has disconnected

Question to discuss:
what would your contemporary art project proposal be
if you were invited by a curator to participate in a
contemporary art exhibition?
Stranger 2: **what?**
Stranger 1: cheese
Stranger 1 has disconnected

Question to discuss:
what would your contemporary art project proposal be
if you were invited by a curator to participate in a
contemporary art exhibition?
Stranger 2: **dunno really**
Stranger 2 has disconnected

Question to discuss:
what would your contemporary art project proposal be
if you were invited by a curator to participate in a
contemporary art exhibition?
Stranger 1: who cares
Stranger 1 has disconnected

Question to discuss:
what would your contemporary art project proposal be
if you were invited by a curator to participate in a
contemporary art exhibition?
Stranger 2: **penis**
Stranger 2 has disconnected

Question to discuss:
what would your contemporary art project proposal be
if you were invited by a curator to participate in a
contemporary art exhibition?
Stranger 1: behind the screen is some twerp
           typing
Stranger 1 has disconnected

Question to discuss:
what would your contemporary art project proposal be
if you were invited by a curator to participate in a
contemporary art exhibition?
Stranger 2: **art**
Stranger 1 has disconnected

Question to discuss:
what would your contemporary art project proposal be
if you were invited by a curator to participate in a
contemporary art exhibition?
Stranger 2: None because I'm a lazy fuck.
Stranger 1: dunno i really dont know much
            about art...
Stranger 2: I'd probably steal someone
            else's.
Stranger 2: More seriously, I don't know,
            maybe a sculpture of a
            character?
Stranger 1: googling contemporary art wait a
            sec
Stranger 2: oh
Stranger 2: that's like
Stranger 2: werid stuff.
Stranger 2: I'd probably make a blank thing
            and call it "the world" for some
            2deep4u stuff.
Stranger 2 has disconnected

Question to discuss:
what would your contemporary art project proposal be
if you were invited by a curator to participate in a
contemporary art exhibition?
Stranger 2: **What**
Stranger 1: no
Stranger 2: **Sorry I don't speak Italian**
Stranger 2 has disconnected

Question to discuss:
what would your contemporary art project proposal be
if you were invited by a curator to participate in a
contemporary art exhibition?
Stranger 2: I would draw
Stranger 2: ink
Stranger 2: black ink
Stranger 1 has disconnected

Question to discuss:
what would your contemporary art project proposal be
if you were invited by a curator to participate in a
contemporary art exhibition?
Stranger 1: what
Stranger 1 has disconnected

Question to discuss:
what would your contemporary art project proposal be
if you were invited by a curator to participate in a
contemporary art exhibition?
Stranger 1: lump of shit and say its about
            womens rights and global
            waarming
Stranger 1: thats pretty much what everyone
            else does right>
Stranger 1 has disconnected

Question to discuss:
what would your contemporary art project proposal be
if you were invited by a curator to participate in a
contemporary art exhibition?

Stranger 1: something in the style of
picasso

Stranger 2: **a hot naked chick standing on a
pedestal**

Stranger 2: **id flow some flowers around the
floor and call it "art"**

Stranger 1: probably analythic kubism

Stranger 2: **omfg art studen**

Stranger 1: lol

Stranger 2: **DUDE**

Stranger 1: those are the only art
defenitions I Know :D

Stranger 1: I study economics

Stranger 2: **hey**

Stranger 2: **I actually would like to ask you
about that**

Stranger 2: **in all seriousness**

Stranger 2: **forget everything I've said
before**

Stranger 1: about what

Stranger 2: **is that a good major?**

Stranger 2: **how easy is it? how quickly can
it be completed**

Stranger 1: well that depends on where you
live, I don't live in America

Stranger 2: **I see**

Stranger 1: However, it should be easy for
everyone to do

Stranger 1: that is, if you're interested in
economics

Stranger 2: **I think economics are boring**

Stranger 2: **do you agree?**

Stranger 1: In my opinion, economics is the
second most usefull major

Stranger 2: **hmmmMmm**

Stranger 2: **but it probably requires you to
take calculus**

94

Stranger 2: right?
Stranger 1: Yes, here we have 56 hours of
            math per semester
Stranger 2: but, there still remains the
            question:
Stranger 2: is it boring?
Stranger 2: it may be useful, but do you
            think it's interesting?
Stranger 1: It's very usefull, but if you
            don't have the feel for it, then
            don't do it because it can be
            quite boring
Stranger 2: do YOU personally think it's
            boring?
Stranger 1: no
Stranger 2: good
Stranger 2: good luck stranger
Stranger 1: thanks, you too
Stranger 2: I have a feeling you will go far
Stranger 2 has disconnected

Question to discuss:
what would your contemporary art project proposal be
if you were invited by a curator to participate in a
contemporary art exhibition?
Stranger 1: idk
Stranger 2 has disconnected

Question to discuss:
what would your contemporary art project proposal be
if you were invited by a curator to participate in a
contemporary art exhibition?
Stranger 1: um
Stranger 1: id draw a line
Stranger 1: and thats it
Stranger 1 has disconnected

Question to discuss:
what would your contemporary art project proposal be
if you were invited by a curator to participate in a
contemporary art exhibition?

Stranger 1: ALL I GOT WAS CONTEMPORARY
PROJECT.
Stranger 1: LOL
Stranger 1: AND.
Stranger 1: ART.
Stranger 1: I'M OUT.
Stranger 1 has disconnected

Question to discuss:
what would your contemporary art project proposal be
if you were invited by a curator to participate in a
contemporary art exhibition?
Stranger 2: **no because moder art sucsk**
Stranger 2 has disconnected

Question to discuss:
what would your contemporary art project proposal be
if you were invited by a curator to participate in a
contemporary art exhibition?
Stranger 1: A dog
Stranger 2 has disconnected

Question to discuss:
what would your contemporary art project proposal be
if you were invited by a curator to participate in a
contemporary art exhibition?
Stranger 2: **jerk off**
Stranger 1: Spray painted bananas.
Stranger 1 has disconnected

Question to discuss:
what would your contemporary art project proposal be
if you were invited by a curator to participate in a
contemporary art exhibition?
Stranger 2: **a freshly-dead body, posed to
make a statement**
Stranger 2: **about the human condition**
Stranger 2: **and about soft drinks**
Stranger 2: **and maybe some brands of
toothpaste**
Stranger 2: **modern art is the biggest
fucking pile of pure shit in the
world**
Stranger 1: well for contemporary art. a
nude painting. oil on canvas.
Stranger 2 has disconnected

Question to discuss:
what would your contemporary art project proposal be
if you were invited by a curator to participate in a
contemporary art exhibition?
Stranger 2: **right**
Stranger 1: your cheese
Stranger 2: **have a good life…**
Stranger 2 has disconnected

Question to discuss:
what would your contemporary art project proposal be
if you were invited by a curator to participate in a
contemporary art exhibition?

Stranger 2: ANAL SEX
Stranger 2: inside a giant rectum
Stranger 1: How would that be an art
            project?
Stranger 1: would you mold a giant anus out
            of clay?
Stranger 1: and shove a clay penis inside of
            it?
Stranger 2: some type of composite
Stranger 2: and the gallery would be inside
Stranger 1: The art gallery would be inside
            the anus?
Stranger 2: inside the rectum
Stranger 1: Are you saying art is shitty?
Stranger 2: Im sure someone would say that
Stranger 1: Haha
Stranger 1: I think a lot of people would
            think that
Stranger 2: Id just do it for the anal sex
Stranger 1: Is that how they would pay you?
Stranger 1: By fucking you in the ass?
Stranger 2: Id pay them
Stranger 1: By fucking them up the ass?
Stranger 2: yea
Stranger 1: Ah ok
Stranger 2: plus Id be sponsored by pysillum
            fiber
Stranger 1: Right because of the anus and
            rectum and all
Stranger 2: u got it
Stranger 2: so can I count on u?
Stranger 1: Should also have free rectal
            exams there too
Stranger 1: with admission
Stranger 2: nice
Stranger 2 has disconnected

Question to discuss:
what would your contemporary art project proposal be
if you were invited by a curator to participate in a
contemporary art exhibition?
Stranger 1: already answered
Stranger 2: **me too**
Stranger 2: **so**
Stranger 2 has disconnected

Question to discuss:
what would your contemporary art project proposal be
if you were invited by a curator to participate in a
contemporary art exhibition?
Stranger 2: ummm
Stranger 1: Idk
Stranger 2: some sort of phot booth project
Stranger 2: photo*
Stranger 1: The others were easy to answer I
just don't know this one
Stranger 1: Asl?
Stranger 2: f21
Stranger 1: Yeah I figured you were a female
Stranger 2: the tits gav it away huh
Stranger 1: :) if only if only
Stranger 2: lol
Stranger 2: a/s?
Stranger 1: M 17 usa
Stranger 2: ah no titty action yet huh
Stranger 1: Hmm depends on what you mean?
Stranger 2: u dont get any action
Stranger 1: C
Stranger 2 has disconnected

Question to discuss:
what would your contemporary art project proposal be
if you were invited by a curator to participate in a
contemporary art exhibition?
Stranger 1: I like trains
Stranger 1 has disconnected

Question to discuss:
what would your contemporary art project proposal be
if you were invited by a curator to participate in a
contemporary art exhibition?
Stranger 1: Something simple and off.
Stranger 2: **welding, lots of welding**
Stranger 1: A green flower, made of copper.
Stranger 1: A green rose.
Stranger 1: Made of copper.
Stranger 2: **sparks and flames**
Stranger 1: "WHY DID HE MAKE IT GREEN? WHY
            IS IT METAL?"
Stranger 1: Nope.
Stranger 2 has disconnected

Question to discuss:
what would your contemporary art project proposal be
if you were invited by a curator to participate in a
contemporary art exhibition?
Stranger 2: **ne dion gardaşş**
Stranger 1: my own shit smeared on a brick
           wall
Stranger 2: **malsn gardaş ne diimm**
Stranger 1: ENGLISH
Stranger 1 has disconnected

Question to discuss:
what would your contemporary art project proposal be
if you were invited by a curator to participate in a
contemporary art exhibition?
Stranger 1: A dick
Stranger 2: **a tiger**
Stranger 1: A giant dick
Stranger 2: **well thats delicious**
Stranger 2: **nice talk**
Stranger 2 has disconnected

Question to discuss:
what would your contemporary art project proposal be
if you were invited by a curator to participate in a
contemporary art exhibition?
Stranger 1: what the fuck is your problem
Stranger 2 has disconnected

Question to discuss:
what would your contemporary art project proposal be
if you were invited by a curator to participate in a
contemporary art exhibition?
Stranger 2: **what**
Stranger 1 has disconnected

Question to discuss:
what would your contemporary art project proposal be
if you were invited by a curator to participate in a
contemporary art exhibition?

Stranger 1: a sheep with no legs

Stranger 2: **I would probably want to do
something along the lines of a
serpentine figure.**

Stranger 1: you can call it the cloud and it
will sell for millions

Stranger 2: **Ehehe**

Stranger 2 has disconnected

Question to discuss:
what would your contemporary art project proposal be
if you were invited by a curator to participate in a
contemporary art exhibition?
Stranger 2: **Spaghetti**
Stranger 2: **Everywhere**
Stranger 1: take a shit on a canvas
Stranger 2: **Shit on a pile of spaghetti**
Stranger 1: than apllies on canvas
Stranger 2: **and put some horsemeat on top
for added relevancy**
Stranger 1: then apllied*
Stranger 2 has disconnected

Question to discuss:
what would your contemporary art project proposal be
if you were invited by a curator to participate in a
contemporary art exhibition?
Stranger 1: what?
Stranger 2: **dog poo**
Stranger 1: dance
Stranger 2 has disconnected

Question to discuss:
what would your contemporary art project proposal be
if you were invited by a curator to participate in a
contemporary art exhibition?
Stranger 2: I might as well be out in space
Stranger 2: Aww yeah
Stranger 2: Hah
Stranger 1: haha no clue
Stranger 2: UP SO CLOSE
Stranger 2 has disconnected

Question to discuss:
what would your contemporary art project proposal be
if you were invited by a curator to participate in a
contemporary art exhibition?
Stranger 2: **something gay**
Stranger 1 has disconnected

Question to discuss:
what would your contemporary art project proposal be
if you were invited by a curator to participate in a
contemporary art exhibition?
Stranger 2: Hmm.
Stranger 2: I don't know.
Stranger 2: Actually.
Stranger 2: I was thinking about this the
other day.
Stranger 2: I'd attach one of those cameras
used for extreme sport to my
chest
Stranger 1: dont think
Stranger 2: Oh?
Stranger 1: just fuck urself?
Stranger 2: Bro.
Stranger 2: That's not cool.
Stranger 1: so
Stranger 2: Why are you so angry? Is there
anything you want to talk about?
Stranger 1: r u female?
Stranger 1: if not sorry
Stranger 2: No, but why are you here to meet
women? Why don't you take a yoga
class,or go to a nightclub? OH
RIGHT, YOU'RE 14 AND LIVE WITH
YOUR PARENTS. SHIT I BET YOU'RE
NOT EVEN IN SHAPE FAGGOT
Stranger 2: ahahaha
Stranger 2: fucking loser kid
Stranger 2: Guess what
Stranger 1: hmhm
Stranger 2: Even after school, you'll still
be a nerd
Stranger 1: nothing
Stranger 2: you might as well kill yourself
now
Stranger 2: do
Stranger 2: it
Stranger 2: please
Stranger 2: I beg of you

Stranger 2: Do us all a favour
Stranger 1: what
Stranger 2: I kind of feel sick that I have
to share this planet with you
Stranger 2: I tell you whaT
Stranger 2: Build and time machine
Stranger 2: and abort yourself
Stranger 1: pardon
Stranger 2: Just end your own life.
Stranger 2 has disconnected

Question to discuss:
what would your contemporary art project proposal be
if you were invited by a curator to participate in a
contemporary art exhibition?
Stranger 1: Not sure.
Stranger 2 has disconnected

Question to discuss:
what would your contemporary art project proposal be
if you were invited by a curator to participate in a
contemporary art exhibition?
Stranger 2: **sleep**
Stranger 1: It would be: do your own
         homework.
Stranger 2: **asl**
Stranger 1 has disconnected

Question to discuss:
what would your contemporary art project proposal be
if you were invited by a curator to participate in a
contemporary art exhibition?
Stranger 1: Again with the same damn
            question
Stranger 2: **i have no idea what kind of**
            vocabulary this is
Stranger 1 has disconnected

Question to discuss:
what would your contemporary art project proposal be
if you were invited by a curator to participate in a
contemporary art exhibition?
Stranger 1: uhh thats hard
Stranger 2: **i dont know i cant even draw a
stickman right**
Stranger 1: that could be your proposal
Stranger 1: "cant draw"
Stranger 1: and then a gallery filled with
sticks
Stranger 2 has disconnected

Question to discuss:

what would your contemporary art project proposal be if you were invited by a curator to participate in a contemporary art exhibition?

Stranger 2: **u male or female**

Stranger 1: i would be art, because who is
        more beauteous than i?

Stranger 1: male

Stranger 2: **i go artk**

Stranger 1: u?

Stranger 2: **same**

Stranger 2 has disconnected

Question to discuss:
what would your contemporary art project proposal be
if you were invited by a curator to participate in a
contemporary art exhibition?
Stranger 2: hmm
Stranger 1: Da booty?
Stranger 2: I think it would involve the use
            of food as modern art
Stranger 2: since I've written on that
            subject before
Stranger 1: Johnlock fan art?
Stranger 2 has disconnected

Question to discuss:
what would your contemporary art project proposal be
if you were invited by a curator to participate in a
contemporary art exhibition?
Stranger 1: Erhm
Stranger 1: I'm a musician
Stranger 1: I once saw a painting in a
            modern art museum called "Black"
Stranger 1: It was a huge canvas painted
            just black
Stranger 1: It was dumb
Stranger 1: Good luck with your art though!
Stranger 1: Bye
Stranger 1 has disconnected

Question to discuss:
what would your contemporary art project proposal be
if you were invited by a curator to participate in a
contemporary art exhibition?
Stranger 2: **dicks dicks everywhere**
Stranger 1: flaccid penis
Stranger 2 has disconnected

Question to discuss:
what would your contemporary art project proposal be
if you were invited by a curator to participate in a
contemporary art exhibition?
Stranger 1: idk
Stranger 2: **penises**
Stranger 1 has disconnected

```
Question to discuss:
```
what would your contemporary art project proposal be
if you were invited by a curator to participate in a
contemporary art exhibition?
```
Stranger 1: I would put mud in a cardboard
            box, throw some glitter on it,
            then cover it in hairspray.
Stranger 2: o rlly
Stranger 1: I totally bet you that some
            idiot will think it's meaningful
            art.
Stranger 2: XD
Stranger 1 has disconnected
```

Question to discuss:
what would your contemporary art project proposal be
if you were invited by a curator to participate in a
contemporary art exhibition?
Stranger 2: **If i understood that i would**
answer
Stranger 2 has disconnected

```
Question to discuss:
```
what would your contemporary art project proposal be
if you were invited by a curator to participate in a
contemporary art exhibition?
```
Stranger 2: Participate
Stranger 2: What the hell
Stranger 2: Sounds sus
Stranger 1 has disconnected
```

Question to discuss:
what would your contemporary art project proposal be
if you were invited by a curator to participate in a
contemporary art exhibition?
Stranger 2: hell no
Stranger 2: modern art sucks
Stranger 1: Modern art really do suck
Stranger 1: But it depends
Stranger 1: is the curator hot?
Stranger 2: yeah i mean if the curator hot
Stranger 1: Does she want the D
Stranger 2: damn
Stranger 2: fuck yeah
Stranger 1: Then fuck the art
Stranger 1: Fuck her
Stranger 2: but then again all fucking
            hipster art bitches are ugly
Stranger 2: dreadlocks
Stranger 2: cheap monday jeans
Stranger 2: herbal tea and all that shit
Stranger 2: converse
Stranger 2: bleh
Stranger 2 has disconnected

Question to discuss:
what would your contemporary art project proposal be
if you were invited by a curator to participate in a
contemporary art exhibition?
Stranger 1: i would go
Stranger 1: with three hot bitches under my
            arms
Stranger 2: **I would spread my ass cheeks**
            then. THat's what modern art is
            now
Stranger 1: a golden cane
Stranger 1: a fur coat
Stranger 1: a purple top hat
Stranger 2: **I would pour spaghetti-o's into**
            my vagina
Stranger 1: take a picture of that with your
            iphone and some old german dude
            will buy it for 2mil
Stranger 2 has disconnected

Question to discuss:
what would your contemporary art project proposal be
if you were invited by a curator to participate in a
contemporary art exhibition?
Stranger 1: Fuckofff
Stranger 1 has disconnected

Question to discuss:
what would your contemporary art project proposal be
if you were invited by a curator to participate in a
contemporary art exhibition?
Stranger 2: **60% of time, it works every time**
Stranger 1: tracy emin
Stranger 1 has disconnected

Question to discuss:
what would your contemporary art project proposal be
if you were invited by a curator to participate in a
contemporary art exhibition?
Stranger 2: hu
Stranger 1: uh
Stranger 2: Brofist
Stranger 1: pewds for life
Stranger 2: Well, i will probably giving a
try spy.
Stranger 1: good luck with that
Stranger 1 has disconnected

Question to discuss:
what would your contemporary art project proposal be
if you were invited by a curator to participate in a
contemporary art exhibition?
Stranger 2: ha?
Stranger 1: What the f***? O.o
Stranger 2: i don't understand
Stranger 2: what kind of proposal?
Stranger 1: Me too
Stranger 1: Maybe we should discuss another
            question.
Stranger 1: What do you prefer boobs or ass?
Stranger 1 has disconnected

Question to discuss:
what would your contemporary art project proposal be
if you were invited by a curator to participate in a
contemporary art exhibition?
Stranger 2: **fuck you on a big piece of paper**
Stranger 1: glue yourself to the wall
Stranger 2 has disconnected

Question to discuss:
what would your contemporary art project proposal be
if you were invited by a curator to participate in a
contemporary art exhibition?
Stranger 2: i'd fling my feces at a canvas
Stranger 2: and call it modern art
Stranger 2: no wait
Stranger 2: i'd let a blind autistic girl
           fling my feces instead
Stranger 2: that'll sell better
Stranger 2 has disconnected

Question to discuss:
what would your contemporary art project proposal be
if you were invited by a curator to participate in a
contemporary art exhibition?
Stranger 1: tomatoes
Stranger 2 has disconnected

Question to discuss:
what would your contemporary art project proposal be
if you were invited by a curator to participate in a
contemporary art exhibition?
Stranger 2: **shit**
Stranger 2: **i'd draw a very complex printed
              circuit**
Stranger 2 has disconnected

Question to discuss:
what would your contemporary art project proposal be
if you were invited by a curator to participate in a
contemporary art exhibition?

Stranger 1: I'd get as many people in the
neighbourhood to ejaculate onto
the walls
Stranger 2: i like sculptures of things made
from other things
Stranger 1: It'd be a collaborative
installation
Stranger 2: hahahaha thats cool too
Stranger 2 has disconnected

Question to discuss:
what would your contemporary art project proposal be
if you were invited by a curator to participate in a
contemporary art exhibition?
Stranger 2: **The best piece of art………. My
dick**
Stranger 1 has disconnected

Question to discuss:
what would your contemporary art project proposal be
if you were invited by a curator to participate in a
contemporary art exhibition?
Stranger 2: **fapping to the oldies**
Stranger 1: Modern violence
Stranger 1: dunno
Stranger 1: weird fetishes
Stranger 2: **so jerking off is modern**
            violence to ones self
Stranger 2 has disconnected

Question to discuss:
what would your contemporary art project proposal be
if you were invited by a curator to participate in a
contemporary art exhibition?

Stranger 1: that doesnt even make any sense
Stranger 2: Ok… I've got nothing!
Stranger 1: english please?
Stranger 2: Does so.. I understand what's
being asked!
Stranger 1: explain
Stranger 2: If you had an Art show… What
would it be about!
Stranger 1: me
Stranger 2: Well of course you!!! LOL
Stranger 2: It's your art how could it not
be about you!!
Stranger 2: What do you want to show
people!! :D
Stranger 1: because im to sexy for an art
show
Stranger 1: i want to show people me
Stranger 2: LOL… Ok… So a show with your
underwear??
Stranger 1: the person reading our
conversation sems like a smart
bitch
Stranger 1: hell yeah
Stranger 1: are you even a guy?
Stranger 2: Bitch??? I don't know…. It seems
to me like they might be
reaching for the finals
presentation
Stranger 2: They can't reply to us!
Stranger 1: your smart to :|
Stranger 1: i know they cant
Stranger 1: how old are you?
Stranger 2: 28… Smart huh??? That really
depends on who you ask!!
Stranger 1: pedo
Stranger 2: Huh??
Stranger 1 has disconnected

Question to discuss:
what would your contemporary art project proposal be
if you were invited by a curator to participate in a
contemporary art exhibition?
Stranger 1: ballsak
Stranger 2: i would show my penis
Stranger 1 has disconnected

Question to discuss:
what would your contemporary art project proposal be
if you were invited by a curator to participate in a
contemporary art exhibition?
Stranger 2: **finally, a question worth
answering**
Stranger 1: Then lets hear it
Stranger 1: I have nothing
Stranger 1: Except maybe some sarcasm
Stranger 1: I'll be nice
Stranger 2 has disconnected

Question to discuss:
what would your contemporary art project proposal be
if you were invited by a curator to participate in a
contemporary art exhibition?
Stranger 2: **puppies**
Stranger 2: **more**
Stranger 1: A giant ball of awesome.
Stranger 2: **puppies**
Stranger 1: With ironic humor.
Stranger 2 has disconnected

Question to discuss:
what would your contemporary art project proposal be
if you were invited by a curator to participate in a
contemporary art exhibition?
Stranger 1: a blank sheet of paper
Stranger 1: I'd title it, "Nothing"
Stranger 2: **blank sheet of paper**
Stranger 2: **tittle it, " close up of albino"**
Stranger 1: LOL
Stranger 1 has disconnected